I0414087

Plain Truth

A reflection upon the country at large amidst the 2016 election

Presented by The Forester

Forward

So here we stand on the precipice of history. Inauguration day for one Donald J. Trump, Winston Churchill and Abraham Lincoln's second worst nightmares coming true before our very eyes. It's not uncommon for dictators to come into power. The difference here is that a majority of the people in this country voted for someone else to be president. There have been presidents elected without a majority. This is the system in which our founding fathers resolved to be in our best interest as a nation. They decided this at a time where there were only 13 states and before any solid political parties were formed. I imagine if they would have known what their creation would have allowed, they would have made plans to come back from the dead before the year 2000 to steer us in a different direction. There are things that have happened in this election never before seen in the history of American elections. No candidate has ever asked another country to hack into our databases and gain information about the other candidate for the purpose of incriminating them. That's a new one. No candidate (at least none that I have studied) has ever publically supported a ruthless dictator. No candidate in recent history has refused to release their tax returns. No candidate has ever been nominated (let alone elected) that has a record of being sued for fraud, and is a pathological liar. There is a difference between a spin doctor and a pathological liar. Donald Trump is simply not capable of telling the truth. This is more a reflection on the electorate on both sides. The combination of lazy voters and voters whose hate runs so deep that it blinds them to the incompetence of who they elected. It's also the electorate's incompetence who believed that a man, with no track record of doing anything positive for anyone, would change their lives for the better. It's a reflection on a group of people who voted for a congressman who assaulted a member of the media on the eve of his election. If they were offended by this in Montana, they certainly have made no attempts to recall him. It's a reflection of a group of people who supported Trump's verbal assault on the media calling them an enemy of the state. It's a reflection on a group of people who are ok with issuing death threats to congressman who attempt to impeach a corrupt president. It's a damning report on about 40% of the American population.

This leaves us at a place in time where the majority of the country is disheartened, disheveled, and in a state of disbelief that this could have happened to our nation. It defies all logic. A slogan of "Make America Great Again" plastered on a cheap hat has captivated the masses. It defies all logic that a country would need to be made great again after 8 years of recovery from the worst recession this country has seen since the Great Depression. The Dow has gone from under 9000, to over 20,000 during the past eight years. The housing market crashed and has since recovered. The American Auto industry was on the verge of extinction and it has made an incredible recovery. We were losing 200,000 jobs a month during 2007 but 11 million have been created under President Obama's watch. Osama Bin Ladin is dead and millions have healthcare that were getting declined because their blood pressure was a little high. I'm curious to know what was so wrong with all that we accomplished that we had to "make America Great Again. "

Some would argue that we've lost factory jobs. Some would argue, and rightfully so, that there are things with Obamacare that need to be fixed. They would also argue that it's an acceptable solution to repeal the entire act without having anything else in place. It could be argued that we did not solve the issues plaguing the Middle East. If fixing these things makes America great again at the expense of going back to the way things were in 2007, it would lead one to believe that the definition of America being great again was defined by people who are clueless as to what being great means to begin with. After all, it was never fully defined during the election by Donald Trump. A group of Americans allowed themselves to be hoodwinked by vague promises with no specific plans on how they would be carried out. They bought into a theory that they were victims of progress and that only Donald Trump could save them. They bought into the theory that they were losing jobs because "Illegal aliens" were taking them. They allowed themselves to believe that the government was responsible for all that is wrong in their lives and expected the government to fix it. They allowed themselves to believe in cartoon characterizations of what Democrats stand for instead of embracing common sense solutions to our nation's greatest challenges.

Our goal is not to seek to change their hearts or reason with this minority group because reason can only be found in an open mind. Our goal must then be to define ourselves to ourselves and prepare to undo the grave injustices that we will undoubtedly take place during the next four years (if he doesn't resign or gets kicked out before then). The injustices, I predict, will be more than social injustices. If the past is any indicator, we will find ourselves with enemies that we once called friends. We will find ourselves economically depressed much to the same tune as we were in 2007. The same conditions that created the recession will now be put back in place. We can only pray that there will be something left to restore when we get back in a position where we can serve the great people of this nation.

Thomas Paine was the author of an essay known as Common Sense. It was a small pamphlet but it sent shockwaves as a call to action for those who believed in the liberty of our fledgling nation. I write this essay in hopes that the shock waves will once again awaken the American people who slept through this past election. In the spirit of Thomas Paine, I'm writing as "The Forester" because the message is much more important than the messenger. The lessons learned in 2000 and 2016 have to be that we cannot become content or complacent. We cannot stand idly by and leave the future of our country to the hands of a sinister dark age. We saw what happened in 2000-2008 when we elected a president who was not up to the task. Unfortunately we may have to endure at least a tenuous four years of a president who has demonstrated that he does not have the emotional intelligence required to succeed in a position where millions of lives depend on stability. Together, we will map out a plan to take on the extremists who are now calling the shots. We will take on those who see no value in the truth. We will take on those who see no value in protecting our senior citizens or those who are less fortunate. We will take on those who choose to align themselves with known dictators and tarnish the good relationships that we have spent years building. The Reckoning begins today.

Who is this book for?

Upon initial reading, one might be under the impression that this is a book by a democrat for democrats. It is true that I am a registered democrat and I make no apologies for that. At the same time, I invite those who consider themselves Independent or even republicans with an open mind to join our cause. If we break down this last election, there is reason to believe that there are enough people who share the same beliefs (at least enough who share the same opposing viewpoints as us) that can make a difference. It starts with the fact that Hilary Clinton won the popular vote by close to 3 million votes. That may sound like a small number but I will put this in perspective. The Indianapolis Motor Speedway has a seating capacity of 350,000. It's 2 and a half miles around. If you've ever attended the Indy 500 you would know full and well just how crowded it is. The margin of victory in the popular vote could have filled up almost 9 Indianapolis Motor Speedways. This was not a small number by any measurement. Donald Trump won 47% of the national vote and out of that 47% I would venture that 30% of those voters were enthusiastic Trump Supporters. Trump does not have the mandate that he believes that he has. There are plenty of reasonable republicans who have denounced him. There are plenty of reasonable republicans who will come to understand that their jobs are in jeopardy if they continue to tie themselves to someone who can become derailed at the slightest hint of criticism. There are initiatives that I will present that they will not agree with totally but I also know that there are items where there is room for discussion. Outside of those like me, who are dyed in the wool democrats, there will be others who will support our cause as a repudiation of a president who knows more about Vladimir Putin than George Washington. I say this with confidence because if he knew anything at all about George Washington, he would understand that an authoritarian has no place in the same office as the man who could have been an authoritarian and chose not to.

This book is for the democrats who have lost their way. I will never believe that the democrats have turned their back on the farmer and the worker. There is too much evidence to prove otherwise. I would be curious to find legislation, however, that proves that the Republican party has somehow picked up where we left off. There are democrats who feel disenfranchised. Democrats who complain that the government doesn't do enough for the auto worker and the coal miner. There are democrats who have somehow decided that Government has impeded their efforts when the reality could not be further from the opposite. There are democrats who feel that someone like a Trump, who caters to the worst of our country, who makes general promises without any specifics, one who puts a slogan on a hat and says that the country isn't great when there is clear evidence that it has improved more under President Obama than any president since FDR. To the impoverished, the disenfranchised, the disillusioned, and those who simply cast a vote because you felt like Trump would solve all your problems, I cordially invite you to come home. Leave your baggage outside. Pick yourself up by your boot straps and get yourself to a better place. If you lost your jobs due to your trade being obsolete, the democrats have made it possible for you to attend school and learn something new about yourself. If you live in a depressed area, as many do in my home state, I invite you to pick up your bags and move. What worked in the past may not be working now. Take the initiative and we will meet you half way.

Where did it all go wrong?

The first thing to understand is that it didn't go entirely wrong. Again, we won the popular vote by almost 3 million. If this were a state election, this essay would not be necessary. The presidential election is the only office where someone can come in first place and still lose. We can debate the merit of the Electoral College all we want but that will not change anytime soon. Our republican friends depend on it as they have only won one popular vote since 1988. Our founding fathers designed a system to where power cannot be concentrated in one area of the country. Whether or not we agree with this system, this is the system we have and must abide for the time being. Having said all that, we still had the majority of the people on our side including every major newspaper in the United States, including every living former president, including several republican leaders. We just happen to fall short in 3 key states who wanted to "try something different". I would submit at this time that if the founding fathers would have known that this system would produce someone like a

George W. Bush or a Donald Trump, they would have never introduced it. Having said that, we must own the fact that we fell short in 3 key states.

So why did we fall short in those 3 key states? This is where the debate picks up. There are several theories, most of which I believe can be debunked. The first one being that jobs were lost overseas. It is true that this is happening but I don't believe for a second that this is what cost us the election. 11 million jobs were added under Obama's tenure. This isn't counting the jobs that came to America from overseas. This was after we lost 200,000 a month during the last year of Bush's tenure. Unemployment is down to 4%. In other words, the job market was white hot. If you did not have a job during the past year it was for one of two reasons…..you didn't want to get a job or you were a one trick pony who couldn't adapt. The internet is a relatively new phenomenon but there has been plenty of advanced notice that technology was going to take over jobs that humans have been doing for decades. Record stores have become all but extinct and have been trending that way since Napster. If you have been paying attention, you would know that you can't walk into a video rental store any longer to rent a movie. If you've been paying attention, you would understand that a successful business can make more of a profit if it gets its products from China. It's now much easier to get products from China. A business owner is in business for one reason and that is to turn a profit. It's not the government's job to bring jobs to you. It is your job to make yourself irreplaceable, valuable, and viable.

The second theory is that there is a mistrust of career politicians. I would agree that corruption does exist in politics. This has been an issue since the founding of our country. No one has ever promised that it will go away. It does not reside solely in one party or the other. I happen to believe that most politicians do go into office with the best of intentions. I don't believe that anyone, on either side, goes in with the intent to bring suffering to the people they represent. I don't believe they go in because they are on a power trip (Unless you admire authoritarians). Our government was intentionally designed to where no one person can have all the power. The characterization of all politicians being corrupt has got to stop with us. We have to be the grown ups who say that while we may not agree with republicans on the issues, most are not bad people.

The Watergate case proved that if corruption is severe enough, both sides will come together to denounce it and deal with it. The Russian hacks proved that Hilary was strategic but not evil. The smoking gun that they claimed they found was the DNC wanting Hilary to be president and not Senator Sanders. While the DNC had their preferences, I don't believe that they cost Bernie the election. I believe that they felt that Hilary had a better chance of winning and acted unskillfully in dealing with that situation. The Republican party has done a great job of convincing a large portion of the electorate that Government is evil and that corporations are people. The government is not an evil foreign entity. It's sole purpose is not to grow like an amoeba and strangle everyone. The government is made up of people, flawed people, but people on both sides who want to represent their constituents. We as a group have to be proud of wanting to produce a government that is of the people, for the people by the people. Participating in our nation's government is a great thing and is to be commended, not frowned upon.

The truth primarily lies in the fact that people did not come out to vote. The numbers are staggering. If the same people who voted for Obama came out to vote, this election would not have been close. We have only ourselves to blame collectively. We believed the polls that said that this would be a landslide for Hilary Clinton. In doing so, we became complacent. We believed that enough people abhorred Donald Trump to the point where there was no fathomable way that he could win the presidency. We were wrong. We underestimated the blind stupidity of a large group of the electorate. www.electoral-vote is one of the more reliable websites as it is very data driven. It has a left wing slant but they are not afraid of reporting the good news along with the bad. They have a spread sheet which shows that democratic turnout was lower by at least 5 percent in Florida, PA, and Michigan. This was enough of a difference to swing these states in Trump's direction. At the end of the day, we have to take responsibility for this and correct it. All 3 of these states had several polls indicating that Clinton would win. All 3 would have been correct had we voted. The fate of the nation can no longer lie in the hands of the pollsters. I predict that we will pay a hefty price for our complacency.

Who Are We?

We find ourselves in the present moment in the middle of an identity crisis. We have lost the presidency. We are a minority in both houses and there are currently more republican governors than democrat governors. This is peculiar given that there is no dispute that there are more registered democrats nationwide and the democrats have won every popular vote except for one since 1988. Some of this can be attributed to gerrymandering, meaning that the districts have been re-drawn to benefit republicans running for the house. The Senate is much closer. Essentially we are 6 seats away from taking it over. In the midst of all this, we find ourselves like a feather in the wind. We're not sure who we need to appeal to. Do we focus our efforts on helping the minority classes knowing that they will be the majority by 2040? Do we put our faith in the old power structure and try to win back the democrats who have lost their way? Do we offer a set of principles and make the attempt to draw everyone toward those principles? Are we obsolete? Do we have anything to offer the American people?

I answer this by submitting that WE are the party of FDR!!! We are the party who pulled this nation out of economic damnation not once but twice. We are the party who made it a priority to take care of our senior citizens by initiating Social Security and Medicare benefits. We introduced Medicaid so that poor people could take care of themselves and their families. We are the party who put a man on the moon! We are the party who said that the US Government has no place in making decisions regarding a woman's right to choose. We are the party who made it possible for everyone to go to college who wanted to go. We are the party who led the charge to kill Osama Bin Laden after Bush Jr was content to let him roam the mountains. We are the party who has been the voice of the voiceless and always have been. The Republican Party likes to bill themselves as the party of Lincoln. They may have hijacked his name but we have his ideals. Lincoln would not be accepted in today's Republican Party but the causes he stood for are very much what the Democrat party stands for today. The republicans left Lincoln when LBJ decided that someone had to stand up for civil rights for all races. The states that are now the blue states are the ones who voted to end slavery and encouraged the government to help the "little guy".

We are the real party of Lincoln! We are the party who said that it was unacceptable to have millions of people not be able to get access to health insurance. We are the party that started Farm Aid to support the average American farmer. We are the party who started the Unions to protect the working man. The survival and success of millions of Americans are by and large a result of Democrats making it happen. Let us never forget that.

When we think about our path forward, we sit at a crossroads. Do we push further to the left or do we try to win back the democrats who have lost their way? My instinct says to gravitate toward the center. We can keep the causes that we love and not sacrifice who we are by working with the Lindsey Grahams and the John McCains of the world who by and large are reasonable people at the end of the day. America tends to always correct itself if it goes too far one way or the other. We've seen this after the economic meltdown of Bush Jr when the democrats took both houses. We saw it swing the other way after the passage of Obamacare. I like the idea of forming a coalition with the reasonable republicans to stand up to the extreme practices of the current administration.

On the other hand, we have two thirds of Americans who support free college tuition even if it means paying higher taxes. We have those who favor universal healthcare if it means paying higher taxes. If there ever was a time to push that far to the left, this next election would be it. We could find out just how far to the left our nation has become but this comes at the risk of Trump getting four more years in the office. We've seen the damage that 8 years of a bad president can do. It took every bit of 6 years of Obama's term to undo the damage that Bush Jr. did during his 8. I don't believe that we can take that risk as the very fabric of our freedom is at stake. What we can do is work with our republican friends, the reasonable republicans, and come up with a plan together that can limit the damage that colleges are allowed to do financially. It really doesn't take $1000 per credit hour per student in a school of 15000 students to run a school especially when you factor in all state allocated funds that they receive anyway. Some might argue that this is the government picking winners and losers. I would argue that if we do nothing, the government would be choosing us as the losers. When you come to understand that most of the nation's wealth is concentrated in the top half of one percent (As

Uncle Bernie says) than you understand that by and large, the government is picking winners and losers with its inaction. Obamacare would be a huge success if we mandated that everyone be on it. Our auto insurance is affordable because the government mandates that everyone have it if you want to drive. If you want to be a citizen in our country, than you must pay in to be a healthy citizen to keep coverage affordable for everyone. That is not an extreme proposition.

I believe that our salvation lies in the center. Again, we do not have to give up our convictions about helping the disenfranchised, about the environment, and about healthcare. Just as it took a coming together of different groups to win our independence, it will take the coming together of two parties to depose someone who has no regard for the constitution, our traditions and our values.

Who is the real enemy?

It's important to understand who the real enemy is here. It's not Republicans in general. It's not Congress. It's not the media, It's not the government. It is the typical Trump supporter. The Trump supporter who voted for him despite the overwhelming evidence that he was unfit, unqualified, and ill tempered. It is the Trump supporter who considers anyone to contradict anything that he does to be a liberal or fake. When challenged, they really can't tell you what it is they have enjoyed thus far in his presidency or his campaign. Is it his treasonous acts of working with Russia to sway the election? Is it his attempts to violate the welfare and safety of the media by calling them fake news and dishonest people? Was it his appointing a secretary of education who has no experience or knowledge of public education? Is it his hiring of an EPA director who wishes to eliminate the EPA? Is it his total disregard for uncontestable facts? What exactly is there to celebrate here? I think to answer this question you have to understand the dynamics at play with this group of ardent Trump supporters.

This is a group that makes up 30 to 40% of the country. Certainly not the majority, but enough to be disruptive. They have always been here but they have been marginalized for many years. There was a period of time throughout the 70's, 80's and even into the 90's where the country did not give air time or attention to these people. There was no Fox News. There was no Rush Limbaugh. These are the uneducated, unsophisticated, and the one dimensional. They are too prideful to be educated while also embarrassed about their lack of education. They hide behind a front of being proud to be unintelligent. Because they don't have an education, they don't have options. They are typically trained in one trade and in constant fear of being replaced by technology or by people who will do their jobs for less money (aka undocumented immigrants). Due to their lack of education or lack of career evolution, they are often doomed to living in poverty. They see no hope of escape and consider themselves to be victims. They don't get to experience different things or different people due to their economic situation so they have a natural fear or resentment of anyone who is different. They consider themselves to be victims. When you consider yourself to be a victim, you will follow the first person to give you an empty promise of hope. Sometimes you truly are a victim to life's circumstances. Sometimes someone comes along who can convince you that you're a victim and that they will be your hope.

Let's revisit the state of Germany during the years immediately following WWI. The Germans were economically depressed. They were held responsible for the events of WWI and were not allowed to have a military. Gone were the manufacturing jobs that supplied the military. Gone was their sense of pride and gone was their prosperity. Along comes a man who promises that he will make Germany great again. He promises jobs, he promises a renewed military and he promises that he can save the German people. He creates scapegoats out of the press. He creates scapegoats out of certain ethnic groups and creates a vision of ethnic purity. He manipulates the truth to fit his narrative and convinces a battered nation that he alone can save them and restore them to the glory of days past. It's a simple message but it works. People are desperate and don't really care to know the details or ask questions. Sound familiar? It's happening here but on a smaller scale. Our nation is actually in very sound financial condition. It's only the people that I described who see America the way the Germans saw Germany during the years between the two great wars who feel that Donald Trump speaks for them. He's proven already that he doesn't care about them but they cling to that hope.

For many years this group had no voice. Say what you will about Rush Limbaugh but the man is a genius. He realized that this group was out there and he catered to them. He found a group that needed confirmation that poor white people were the oppressed minority in this nation. Rush was essentially a Lone Ranger until Fox News came along and built a supporting cast. Fox News deserves a lot of credit for galvanizing what I call the 40 percenters and turning them into a political movement which has produced chaos and turmoil in our elections.

What needs to be understood by these people is that Trump has no intention of helping them. They were essentially a pawn for him to win an election. His credibility has been blown time and again so there is no reason to believe a word that he says. This is the track record of lies that one would expect from a pathological liar and a sociopath....

- There were hundreds of muslims dancing in the streets of New Jersey during 9/11
- He claimed it wasn't him who called into a radio show acting as a PR person representing Donald Trump. He denied this at first, later admitted that it was him, and then denied it again years later.
- He wants everyone to buy American but his clothes are made in China. He tried to deny this on the Letterman show.
- He said during the debate that he did not know Putin but said a few years earlier that the two had met on occasion.
- He claimed the pipeline would be made with American Steel. He's ordering it from China.
- He claims that thousands engaged in voter fraud
- He claimed that he had the most electoral votes since Reagan which is totally false
- He claimed that he had more people at his inauguration than Obama, another lie
- He claimed that Mexicans were essentially invading our country when immigration is at its lowest point in over a decade
- Claimed that President Obama wire tapped his hotel

- He said that Ted Cruz's father killed JFK
- Said that three accused black students were guilty of assault even though they were cleared with DNA evidence. He took out an ad in a newspaper to render his verdict
- Said that Obama was a muslim from Kenya with any evidence
- Trump said that he never said he was in favor of toppling Gaddafi while there is video evidence of the contrary
- Trump said that he was for universal healthcare on 60 minutes before deciding he was against it
- He was pro-choice before he was pro-life
- He was for the Iraq Invasion before he was against that

There is no lack of evidence to convict Trump of being a serial liar or a perverted human being for that matter. The New York Times was able to fill up an entire page with lies that Donald Trump has told since campaigning. The fact that anyone, let alone a majority population of entire states, would put their trust in someone who is a known liar is deeply disturbing. What's more disturbing is the fact that they didn't vote for Trump but rather voted against Hilary. I was not Hilary's biggest supporter but looking at both candidates logically, there was no contest as far as who was better qualified to lead a government. We now stand in a situation where truth doesn't matter. Civility does not matter. The first amendment doesn't matter. The only thing that matters is winning. Think about this, their hatred for democrats run so deep that they would support a candidate in Montana who assaulted a journalist. They sent death threats to congress people in Texas who proposed impeachment. A group in one of the southern states intimidated a female congressional candidate into dropping out of the race. It doesn't matter what gets accomplished or does not get accomplished. It doesn't matter who gets hurt in the process even if they get hurt. The only thing that matters is winning. When you get to this point where one of the two major parties would support a man who exhibits sociopathic traits, it sets our fundamental system of government up to be fragile at best. These people are political kamikazes. Elections going forward will not be about democrat vs republican but more so along the lines of the government of our founding fathers vs. the government of deceit, lies, and authoritarianism. The republicans will tell you that they are the party of our founding fathers but there is no founding father that would be ok with a foreign country interfering in our elections. They believed in the truth while this republican party has abandoned it. They would not have been ok with restricting the press, not allowing people into our country based on race and making false accusations against former presidents. This is why I can definitively say that the 40 percenters cannot be counted as the party of the founding fathers. How do you know if you're in this 40%? I'll give you a few hints.

- You claim to be for less government but support a man who admires Vladamir Putin
- You listen to Alex Jones and Sean Hannity and think that they, in any way shape or form, make a valid point on anything.
- You support a health care bill that guts Medicaid
- If you at any point wore a Paul Revere outfit to a rally
- If you believe that the government should be run like a small business
- If you are worried about "Illegal Mexicans" taking your job
- If you watch CNN and think that Jeffrey Lord and Kelly Anne Conway are smart and witty

- If you like Trump because he "Tells it like it is"

This is the side of our country that must be isolated. The unreasonable side, the irrational side, the side that fears science and facts. Now let's talk about Republicans who aren't the enemy. I'm reaching out to those who like their guns but who also believe in Medicaid for their poor relatives who got this way through no fault of their own. I'm reaching out to the republicans who don't encourage abortion but who don't believe in the government being able to dictate what a woman can do with her own body. I'm reaching out to Republicans who value truth and reject the Kelly Ann Conways, the Jeffrey Lords, the Sarah Palins, and all others who flat out have difficulty with presenting facts in an accurate manner. We want you with us.

How Dangerous is this man?

Is Donald Trump Hitler? No. He does not have the means or the social conditions present to commit the atrocities that Hitler committed. What cannot be ignored are the characteristics that he possesses which would lead someone to believe that he admires totalitarian dictators such as a Hitler, a Stalin, a Putin, a Kim Jung Un and the like. He has no problem with making pronouncements and declarations that are false. He has no problem with banning people from certain countries from entering the United States, even if they have a legal Visa. He has exhibited racially charged behavior throughout his life. He was a part of a lawsuit to where he denied African Americans residency in one of his apartment complexes even though they were qualified to live there. I have not seen where the illegal immigrants that he is rounding up are anything other than those from Mexico and other countries south of our boarder. He's not chasing after illegal Canadians or Europeans. He is a classic European sympathizer in the sense that he admires traits of European dictatorships which led to two world wars. He has no issues with overstepping freedom of the press. By willfully ignoring facts, he can create his own reality. This is a reality that revolves around him alone and he can totally control it. These are all traits of a classic narcissist. If being president required passing a lie detector test and a psychological evaluation, he would not be allowed anywhere near the office. He has essentially politicized the economy. He chooses winners and losers (which makes him a socialist) and he has created an environment where the worst that our country has to offer is enabled. At the end of the day, however, he is not all that dangerous…..yet. All of his foreign leader conversations have one underlying theme and that is aggression. He has threatened China, Mexico, Iran, Australia, North Korea and is not welcome in the House of Commons. If you believe that we exist as an island unto ourselves, than this would be acceptable. The problem is that we can't. Even if we could, it's never a good idea to have every major world power against you. He clings to Vladamir Putin as if he is a mirror image of himself. Putin will no doubt turn on Trump as he has on every other US President since taking office. The one thing to remember at the end of the day is this……he is one man. Try as he might to undermine the judicial branch, there are enough advocates of checks and balances in this country to maintain our fundamental systems of liberty set forth by the founding fathers. From the very beginning, George Washington deferred to Congress even when he didn't have to. He had all the support to be a dictator, yet he had enough vision to put power into the hands of the people. We are a Representative Republic for a reason. In due time, Congress will either have to restrain Trump's ruthless aggression through impeachment or risk losing their seats. They understand, at the end of the day, that there were over 3 million people who voted for someone other than Donald Trump. This is not lost on them. Congress would be wise to assert their authority now while the White House is operating under pure Chaos. When a White House Sr. Advisor admonishes the press and the public with words indicating that the President is not to be questioned, this should be considered as a shot across the bow and a direct attack on our fundamental system of government. Yes, we are a two party system but there have always been fundamental agreements on what values initiated by the founding fathers should remain unscathed. Checks and Balances are where the line must be drawn and action must be taken.

Where we stand

We are less than 6 months into this Presidency. During this month we have had allegations of Russia spying and attempting to influence our elections. We have a President saying that we are the moral equivalent of Russia. We have a Sr. Advisor resigning due to leaking intelligence to Russia. We have an Attorney General who lied about a question that he wasn't even directly asked during his confirmation hearing. It turns out that even he had contacts with Russia. We have a president who has accused his predecessor of wire tapping. You have a director of the EPA who wants to eliminate the EPA. You have a secretary of energy who knows nothing about nuclear energy. You have a Secretary of Education who knows nothing about public education. You have a republican congress who wants to wipe out a health care system that provided 18 million people with insurance who would not have had it otherwise. You have a congress who refuses to stand up to a president that they secretly believe is insane out of fear that they will alienate the 30% who approve of the lies, deceit, and corruption.

The Electoral College

The electoral college must be abolished. We've had two situations in sixteen years where the will of the people was not honored. Two situations where the majority of the people voted for one candidate and the other candidate was given the presidency of the United States. This does not happen in any other election, period. I've studied the electoral college in depth (One of the perks of being a history major) and I cannot find where there ever has been or ever could be a justification for a second place contender to be deemed a winner. The closest justification that I can find is that this was an easier and more efficient way to tally results rather than to have to wait for every single vote to be counted. The process of tallying every single vote would have taken far too long during the late seventeen/early eighteen hundreds. States would be awarded "points" based on population. Once that state had enough returns to determine a winner, those points (so called electors) would be awarded. It was efficiency, no more and no less. The electoral college was also established during a time when there were no political parties. If there had been several candidates running for president, the winner of the popular vote would not necessarily have a majority support from the country. The electoral college was a way to establish a winner take all approach in the states so that the House would not have to decide the presidency. We now live in a time where we can tally votes faster than ever. We live in a time where a super majority of the votes go to one of the two major parties. No third party candidate has a realistic chance of impacting the popular vote. The electoral college is not necessary, it is out of date, and it has proven to be dangerous to our country. We need look no further than the 8 years of George W. Bush to prove this. The people voted against him and for good reason. For those who believed that he was a good president, I ask you to look at his approval rating when he left. Republicans were running away from George W. Bush as if he was on fire. The economy had crashed. The housing market had crashed. The auto industry had crashed. The job market had crashed. Thousands of our finest men and women died to chase down weapons of mass destruction that didn't exist. All the while, Bin Ladin was running in the Mountains of Afghanistan. We have the electoral college to thank for all that. The electoral college has once again contributed to an incompetent leader being in a position that he has no business being in. In fact, the Republican presidential candidates have won the popular vote once since 1988. Think about this, one time, since 1988, more people voted for a republican than a democrat. The argument that republicans make in favor of the electoral college is that it prevents one or two states from having all the power. I don't buy this for a second. In essence the argument should be that the electoral college gives more power to smaller states instead of reflecting the will of the entire nation which is what an election should do. This is what Washington envisioned when he presided over the Constitutional convention. It would take a monumental power shift to abolish the electoral college but we do have enough people to do it. It's just a matter of everyone voting in their state elections.

The Road to Recovery – First step, your back yard.

There are two ways that we can address the issues at hand. One is to let things hit rock bottom. We can sit back and let people feel the totality of their actions by letting them suffer because of the decisions that they made at the voting booth. We could allow them to repeal Obamacare. We could allow the 18 million who had coverage to lose it. We can allow our seniors to see a 75% increase in their premiums. They would live in a world where they can't afford to retire. We could allow public schools to be a thing of the past. We could allow mass deportations of those whose only crime was wanting a better life for their families. We can allow Trump to continue to promise one thing and do another in regards to those manufacturing jobs that he promised to bring back while he imports steel from China. We can allow the press to be abused and the first amendment to be assaulted. We can allow jobs to disappear and the dow to sink 6000 points while we go back to the good ole days of 2008. We don't have to push to win the mid terms and we don't even have to challenge

Trump for his re-election. It took George Bush JR 6 years for everything that he and his congressional colleagues to take shape. Maybe it's just not that bad yet. Maybe we could wait……..maybe.

The other option would be to understand that there are 3 million more people who voted for someone other than Donald Trump for President and do something about it. Understand that we lost the electoral college vote by less than 100,000 people. It wasn't the Trump voters who won the election for him. It was the voters who stayed home who won it for him. What we cannot have, going forward, is an apathetic electorate. The rumble that will reach Washington D.C has to begin as a tremor on the local level. It starts with voting for those elections that you don't believe mean anything. We have to start flipping our state legislatures and our governors. This will be easier to do in some places than others but I guarantee you that once the house sees that they are in jeopardy, they will begin to panic. The other thing that needs to happen is getting people to the polls. If you have friends who are democrats, you need to physically pick them up and take them to the voting station. 2018 is so important. We can undo the gerrymandering which has made it possible for Republicans to have the majority in the house. 2018 is the year where we can vote out the Mitch McConnells and the Rand Pauls who do nothing but take up valuable space and who do not represent the common man. 2018 will be our last great hope for many years and we absolutely must make it count.

To win in 2018 there are some issues that we must take the lead on. Trump won in part because he controlled the narrative of the debate. He was allowed to make the election about things that most people simply did not care about. I don't care what anyone says, a majority of Americans could care less about Nafta. Illegal immigration may have been an issue on the border states but the fact is that it was down by 50% before Donald Trump won the election. Hillary spent her time attacking Trump's character (and rightfully so) and having to defend herself amidst the email allegations. We cannot run another campaign like this. Trump is a terrible person but you won't convince his base that. The truly independent voters are few and far between. A truly independent person would see that Trump is a mentally unstable human train wreck and not vote for anyone remotely related or attached to him. What we need to do is play to our strengths. We need to preach the gospel of the economy that we created during the Obama and Clinton years. We've earned the right to brag about this. We've earned the right to brag about 4% unemployment because we created the conditions that made this possible. We are the party who cares about education and will provide a future for the children of our country. This is a gospel that we've earned the right to preach! We will address the issues that republicans refuse to address. The republicans have been silent on public education. They have been a flat out threat to the fundamental nature of our healthcare. We want to fix it, they simply want to destroy it. When you think about what most people want, it's very simple......

1. They want jobs so they can keep a roof over their heads
2. They want access to healthcare when they are sick
3. They want their children to have a future
4. They want to be left alone

We are more than qualified, more than capable to take care of all four of these things. These are the items that we must campaign on. Campaign and win we will!!!!!

What the Republicans lost when they won the election

- They lost the right to be offended by any sexual indiscretions by any democrat running for office.
- They lost the right to be offended by sexually explicit language
- They lost the right to complain about congressional spending as soon as they decided that it was ok to spend trillions on building a wall.
- They lost the right to complain about threats to the president when Ted Nugent threatened to kill Obama and Hillary. The right stood by and did nothing.
- They lost the right to complain about any democrat who switches positions on any given policy

- They lost the right to blame everything on a liberal media when their president won without it.
- They lost the right to complain when democrats exercise the nuclear option to appoint supreme court justices
- They lost the right to complain about any candidate being too much of a celebrity
- They lost the right to claim that government should be run like a business
- They lost the right to ever try to take away healthcare or medicare from those in need
- They lost the right to claim that they are the party of the common man when they decided it was ok to double down on trickle down.
- They lost the right to complain about anything that any future first lady wears considering this first lady has been photographed wearing nothing.

The republicans, by standing by a dictator in training, have rendered themselves permanently irrelevant. They are not the party of the common man. They are not the party of Abraham Lincoln. The republicans led us into the greatest financial disaster that we have seen since the 1930's. I cannot point to any major legislative successes that they have had as a party in recent times outside the prescription plan for Medicare.

The republican party would like to think that this past election was a referendum on Hillary Clinton. Hillary Clinton, despite her flaws, won the popular vote by more than 3 million people. This was no reflection of Hillary Clinton. It is, however, a reflection of the type of candidate that a republican would support. They would support a guy who has a history of bullying based on sex and race. They supported a guy who bankrupted a casino and said that he was a "good business man". They supported someone who was pro-choice until he decided he was a republican. They supported someone who out right lied about trivial things after claiming they didn't vote for Kerry because he was a "Flip Flopper". They voted for a man who disguised his voice on a phone call in order to brag about himself while acting like another person. They voted for a guy who single handedly brought down an entire football league! They voted for a man who has done nothing but lie, and lie some more since being elected. They voted for a guy who said Hillary should have gone to jail for mishandling classified information, who then turned around and gave classified information to Russia. They voted for a man who refused to disclose his tax forms. They voted for a man who psychologists have determined to be a narcissist and someone who's mental abilities have declined significantly during the last decade. This is a reflection of the republican party....a party who every time is entrusted to govern fails and fails miserably. This is testimony to the character of the current Republican Party.

The art of Governing

We've spent quite a bit of time discussing why the republicans don't deserve power. Getting power isn't the toughest end of the equation, keeping it is. There are things that we as democrats can do to keep power once we are in the majority. There is nothing more dangerous to an incumbent than an energized base. We can't continue to only push our agenda and ignore the wishes of the voters. We must find out their needs and reach a compromise where we can. I know that compromise has become a dirty word because it's been associated with selling out. This is especially true on the right. They have been so busy obstructing that they have forgot how to govern. Our current congressman forget that our country was founded upon the very principal of compromise. We would not have a bi-cameral government but not for "The Great Compromise". The Civil War would have visited sooner upon us but not for the various compromises that bought precious time. Compromise is very possible. The 40% who would support a candidate like Trump can be isolated if the remaining 60% can agree to compromise. You may be asking ' How did he come up with 40%'. If you look at Trump's approval ratings before the election up to the present time, he tends to hover around that 40% mark. His rating was as high as 47% on election night. It didn't take long for 7% of his voters to realize he has no clue about governing and is a pathological liar. He's actually closer to 35% but I'm going to go with the average. The fact that there are 40% in this country who would support anyone like a Donald Trump is alarming. This is a reflection on their values. Their values dictate that it's ok to lie almost 100% of the time. It's ok to cut health insurance (even for their own neighbors) because it's a republican idea and not a government. You cannot compromise with people who's values are that out of line with generations of Americans. These are people who value dictatorships as they voted for a man who wants to be like Putin. On the other hand, Trump has presented an opportunity for those who are willing to compromise to stand up and be accounted for. The reasonable members of the republican wing have drawn their lines in the sand. We needed to get to this point. For eight years, there was no line. It's refreshing to hear John Boehner talk like a reasonable human being after he took off his republican uniform. The two uniforms going forward can only be the uniform for those of us who believe in the same constitution as Washington and Madison and the uniform that represents oppression, stupidity, and blind obedience.

The democrats, supported by the reasonable group of republicans, will take back power. When this happens, there will have to be some basic understandings. The next great compromise will have to be on two issues that must remain off the table. Those issues are second amendment rights and abortion rights. We, as democrats, must agree that we will not push any agenda to restrict gun rights. I know this is controversial, but hear me out. We're in a situation where the NRA propaganda machine has convinced a majority of gun owners that a ban on one type of gun is a ban on all guns. In theory, if the government has the capacity to ban one, they can ban them all. It's a terrible theory because it would be political suicide if the democrats did somehow pull this off. Most democrats (excluding those on the extreme left) have no issues with gun ownership in general. I know plenty of democrats who like to hunt and who like the idea of protecting their home. The issue comes down to limiting certain types of guns for certain types of people. Could a psychopath get their hands on an automatic weapon? Sure. Legislation could not stop this. Legislation also does not stop drinking and driving but we can prove that it has cut down on the number of drinking and driving fatalities. I digress. The point is no matter how much logic is used to tackle this issue of gun violence, we will never have the political wherewithal to alter the gun control landscape. That change has to come from within. We have to accept this as one part of the compromise. The other aspect of the compromise is abortion rights. The Republican party will never have the political wherewithal to alter a woman's right to choose. We must compromise to make change where we can but accept those areas that are non-negotiable at this point. This is going to be the best way to maintain power once we achieve it.

The changing political landscape

Political parties have changed several times over the course of our young country. We've had the Democrats, the Republicans, The democratic-republicans, the Whigs, the Free-Masons and Free Soil parties. We've even had a president elected from the Bull Moose party. The Democrats and Republicans have had a great run for over 150 years. This rivalry was largely based on geography. It was the North vs the South. As the country expanded, many other pockets formed. The Republican party was a valuable asset to a large group of people. Now it's not so much a geographic rivalry as it is an ideological rivalry. States went to Trump that have not voted republican In decades. In my humble opinion, I won't be surprised to find out that Russia did indeed flip states that Trump should not have won. When your margin of victory is 88000, it leaves room for doubt. It doesn't change the fact that our divisions now are primarily ideological. The question then becomes how relevant one party is over the other. If you look at it strictly by the facts, it's not even close. The Republican party has won one popular vote since 1988. If there was no electoral college, George Bush Sr would have been our last republican president. The republican presidents by and large were a stable group until Herbert Hoover sent us into the great depression. Since that time, I can only count one Republican president who was productive and that was Dwight Eisenhower. We all know how Nixon fared. Ford stumbled into the presidency. Reagan was more of a democrat than a republican. Bush Sr led us into an economic meltdown. Bush Jr led us into the worst economic crisis since the great depression. Then there's Trump. Not exactly a resume of success. Republicans in congress were productive until close to the year 2000. I'll take the economy that we had under Joe Scarborough and John Kasich. Since then, it's been nothing but whining about the media, obstructionism, and more whining about the media. The republican party, as dominated by the 40%, is irrelevant. They will continue to strive for power but I don't feel that they should be allowed to do it under the Republican banner. They don't represent democratic values nor really anything that Lincoln stood for. We are essentially 3 separate parties. A coalition government of the middle and the left can do great things for this country. We can return to a country that values facts, that rejects hatred of minorities and those who choose to be educated. We can be a country where there can be a balance between fiscal conservatism and being our brother's keeper. There is room between the left and the middle to make America great again!

Common Sense

I go back to some of the points made in Thomas Paine's heroic essay 'Common Sense'. The points that he made back then can certainly be applied to the issues of this day. We determined that it did not make sense that the US being a larger country would be dominated by a small country thousands of miles away. We can say today that it does not make sense that an overwhelming majority of democrats should be dominated by a smaller number of republicans simply because more democrats choose to live along the coasts and in the North. It's only common sense that the majority who benefits from Obamacare would not be dominated by a minority who wants to take insurance away from over 20 million people. It does not make sense that the needs of the many should take second tier to the needs of the elite few who aren't willing to pay their fair share of taxes. Another person who believed in these ideals was George Washington himself.

There are four things, which I humbly conceive are essential to the well being, I may even venture to say, to the existence of the United States, as an Independent Power–

- 1st An indissoluble Union of the States under one federal Head.
- 2dly A sacred regard to public Justice.
- 3dly The adoption of a proper Peace Establishment, and
- 4thly The prevalence of that pacific and friendly disposition among the People of the United States, which will induce them to forgit their local prejudices and policies, to make those mutual concessions which are requisite to the general prosperity, and in some instances, to sacrafice their individual advantages to the interest of the Community.

These are the Pillars on which the glorious Fabrick of our Independency and National Character must be supported–Liberty is the Basis, and whoever should dare to sap the foundation or overturn the Structure, under whatever specious pretexts he may attempt it, will merit the bitterest execration, and the severest punishment which can be inflicted by his injured Country.

The fourth pillar speaks volumes as to what Washington's vision was for these United States. Notice that he says "Forgit their local prejudices and policies to make those mutual concessions". There can be no mistaking his message. The current Republican party is clearly placing local prejudices above the needs of the entire nation. Do what is right by George Washington and sacrifice your individual advantage so that the interests of the nation can be maintained. Don't tell us that the interests of our nation lies in taking Medicaid away from our most disenfranchised.

Recessional

I appreciate your taking the time to listen to the thoughts and musings of one man who loves and believes in his country. As I write, the economy is still strong. Our foundations are still in place. The one good thing about a Trump presidency is that he has provided the greatest test to the strength of our democracy that we have seen since the Civil War. Despite his being a sociopathic liar, despite his catering to the worst that our country has to offer, despite his attempts to integrate a dictatorship with our democracy, our young nation still stands. I predict that he will be impeached. I predict that we will find that he directed his staff to work with Russia. I predict that we will find that Russia did indeed find a way to sway votes which caused Clinton to lose Michigan, Florida, and PA by one percent. Remember, they only needed to sway 3 states out of 50. This is the flaw in our electoral college system that must be addressed and I predict it will. We will be given the opportunity to right the wrongs and we will take advantage of that opportunity without fail. Anyone who supported this president will be punished by history. An entire party could fall if they do not do the right thing and thoroughly denounce Trump just like a few of the brave republicans have. We cannot have elections won by people who physically assault their opposition, intimidate and threaten candidates who choose to run, or threaten to imprison their opponents. The moral arch of our nation is long but it will not stand for this type of oppression. Everyone who is not a part of the 40% Unite!!! Pick up the pieces and move forward. For those who don't believe that those on the right will do the right thing, don't you be weary. At the end of the day he is just one man. One spoke on the wheel of democracy which will be replaced in due time. Stay strong America!!!! In the words of the iconic Winston Churchill…..

" You have only to persevere in order to conquer. At the end of the road, be it short or long, victory and honor shall be yours."

www.ingramcontent.com/pod-product-compliance
Lightning Source LLC
Chambersburg PA
CBHW071130280526
45787CB00003B/1236